WELCOME TO HMS VICTORY

On 7 May 1765 a magnificent new ship of the line was floated out of the Old Single Dock in Chatham's Royal Dockyard. She was HMS *Victory*, a first-rate battleship and the largest and most up-to-date ship in King George III's Royal Navy. In the years to come, over an unusually long service, she would gain renown leading fleets in the American War of Independence, the French Revolutionary War and the Napoleonic War. She achieved lasting fame as the flagship of Vice-Admiral Lord Nelson in Britain's greatest naval victory, the defeat of the French and Spanish at the Battle of Trafalgar.

It is almost impossible today to imagine the physical brutality of fighting at sea in sailing warships. These great wooden battleships, under acres of sail, confront each other at point blank range, their crews intent on smashing and capturing the other ship. Their heavy guns blasted tons of iron, shattering hulls, splintering masts and yards, overturning gun carriages and filling the air with deafening noise and blinding smoke.

She may seem beautiful to our eyes, but *Victory* was built ___ as a huge and complex mach___ ___ every man in her ___ in operating ___ imately she ___ ___ to fire her ___ or iron shot.

'A man should witness a battle in a three-decker from the middle deck, for it beggars all description; it bewilders the senses of sight and hearing.'

(Lewis Roatley, *Victory*'s 2nd Marine Lieutenant, aged 20)

A New Battleship

In 1758 Britain was at war with France; the conflict would last for seven years and be fought all round the world, in North America, the Caribbean, the Mediterranean and India.

The war, especially in its early years, was fought at sea, so a decision was taken in December 1758 to build 12 new 'ships of the line'. One of these was to be an unnamed 'first-rate ship', that is a battleship carrying at least 100 guns, and the largest ever ordered for the Royal Navy.

This decision, with its great cost, was not taken lightly. The new first-rate ship would cost £63,176 and three shillings – not a large figure today when an equivalent capital ship costs billions of pounds, but a huge sum at the time. The decision was so important that when *Victory*'s keel, the backbone of the ship, was laid down on 23 July 1759 the occasion was marked by a visit from Prime Minister William Pitt.

The newly ordered first-rate was only given the name *Victory* on 13 October 1760. Up to that date there had been five other vessels with the name, the previous *Victory*, also a first-rate ship, having been lost off the Channel Islands with all hands in 1744. After her sinking some felt the name 'Victory' was a bad omen, but as Britain was again at war and had just enjoyed a year of famous naval victories in 1759, the name was thought appropriate. *Victory* has remained a Royal Navy ship ever since, and still serves as the flagship of the Commander-in-Chief Naval Home Command.

Left: Admiral George Anson was First Lord of the Admiralty when the decision to build HMS *Victory* was taken.

Left: The Battle of Quiberon Bay (20 November 1759) remains one of the greatest victories ever obtained by the Royal Navy and helped to create the idea of the Annus Mirabilis – Year of Miracles.

Throughout this period the Royal Navy's principal fighting ships were 'rated', from sixth- to first-rates according to the number of guns. A sixth-rate was a frigate with 24 to 28 guns, whilst third-rates with 74 to 80 guns were the typical size for 'ships of the line', those ships large enough to fight in a fleet battle. First-rate ships were more powerful still: with an extra gun deck and 100 guns or more, they were the largest moveable man-made objects of their time.

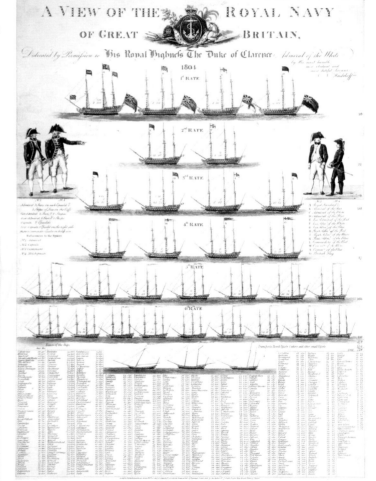

BUILDING HMS VICTORY

Victory was built in a specially prepared dry dock at Chatham to a design by Sir Thomas Slade, the Surveyor of the Navy. The design was not new, but followed the lines of the *Royal George* completed three years earlier. Over 250 skilled shipwrights worked on her hull, using timbers from around 2,000 oak trees which had been felled in Sussex and Kent years before.

Once the timbered frame of the *Victory* was completed, it was covered and the wood allowed to season for a period in dry dock. She was actually left for three years – much longer than was usual – before work to finish and fit her was resumed in 1763. This long seasoning of her great oak timbers may be one reason she has survived so long.

When *Victory* was finally 'launched' (towed out of the flooded dock) in May 1765 the Seven Years War had finished and there was no immediate role for her. So, like many other ships, she spent a full 12 years covered and moored in the River Medway until she was called to fight in a new war against the old enemy France. On 13 April 1778, painted a distinctive red and flying the flag of Admiral Augustus Keppel, she finally made sail from Chatham to join the Channel Fleet and defend Britain against invasion.

Right: HMS *Victory* as she appeared when completed for sea in 1778.

Below: Sir Thomas Slade, Britain's greatest naval architect of the 18th century and designer of HMS *Victory*.

THE GREAT REPAIR

After 1797 the battle-weary *Victory* was considered unfit for service and was fitted out to become a hospital ship. However, in 1799 HMS *Impregnable* was lost and the fleet needed a replacement first-rate ship. This led to the three-year refit known as the 'Great Repair', which turned out to be more extensive than expected. *Victory*'s open stern galleries were closed in, two extra gun ports were added to the Lower Gun Deck, and the heavy 42-pound guns on this deck were replaced with lighter 32-pounders, whilst her magazines were lined with copper. Above decks her original ornate figurehead was changed to a much simpler design and her masts were replaced.

Above and below: Chatham Dockyard. The Royal Dockyards were amongst the largest industrial complexes in the world during the late 18th and early 19th centuries. When launched in 1765, *Victory* was immediately placed 'in ordinary' and moored in the river Medway, just off the dockyard where she was constructed.

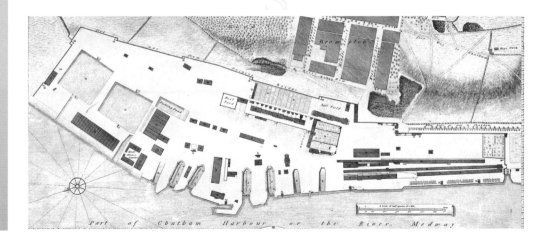

Victory's History, 1778–1800:

1778	fights in the inconclusive first Battle of Ushant
1780	'middling' repair at Portsmouth, copper sheathing fitted to *Victory*'s bottom for the first time
1781	under Admiral Richard Kempenfelt, captures an entire convoy of troopships from under the noses of their French escorts at Ushant
1782	under Admiral Richard Howe, in action off Cape Spartel and at the Relief of Gibraltar
1793–4	flagship of the Mediterranean Fleet under Admiral Lord Hood for the attack on the main French arsenal at Toulon
1795	took part in the unsuccessful action off Hyères and had to withdraw to Lisbon
1797	flagship of Admiral Sir John Jervis, who led *Victory* with 14 ships against a Spanish fleet of 27 at the Battle of Cape St Vincent
1797–9	fitted as a hospital ship

THE POOP DECK, QUARTER DECK AND FORECASTLE

The short Poop Deck at the stern (the word 'poop' comes from the Latin *puppis*, meaning rear) is the highest on the ship and was used as a viewpoint and signalling platform. The signal flags were stored here and, high up, three huge lanterns burned whale oil to give a bright light and show the *Victory*'s position.

Directly below the Poop Deck are the Captain's Quarters, with a Dining Cabin, Day Cabin and a Bed-place. The Dining Cabin has a sliding skylight and this was the only place that Captain Hardy at 6ft 4ins tall could stand upright.

The Quarter Deck, immediately outside the Captain's Quarters, was the ship's nerve centre. Officers directed operations from here. Under the overhang of the Poop Deck were the ship's wheel and compass binnacle, essential for steering and navigation. The *Victory*'s

Master, and the Admiral's Secretary, occupied small cabins on either side of the ship's wheel.

The Forecastle, or Foc'sle, is a short area of deck at the bow where the ship's bell and sandglasses were housed. These regulated the crew's working day, the bell being rung every half hour until eight bells marked the end of a four-hour watch. The Foc'sle has four guns, two of which are the 'carronades' nicknamed 'the Smasher', which could fire a massive 68-pound shot at short range.

Sails and spars were operated from here and anchors lowered, raised and stowed. The 'Gangboard' gave direct access to the bowsprit, but it was more usually called 'Marines' Walk' because a marine would be stationed here whilst in port to ensure men did not desert.

Far left: A 68-pounder carronade. *Victory* was the only ship at Trafalgar equipped with this weapon. These relatively short but powerful guns sent a 68-pound shot smashing through an enemy's hull with devastating effects at close range.

Far left: The log line and reel, used to measure the ship's speed. The log line itself is knotted every 47ft 3ins. With the log dropped into the sea, the line ran over the stern and the knots were counted against a time glass. The number of knots counted in 28 seconds gave the ship's speed.

Left: Signal flags were stored in a locker on *Victory*'s Poop Deck.

At 11.45 on the morning of 21 October 1805, after the British fleet had been warned to prepare for battle, Nelson summoned Flag Lieutenant John Pasco and told him he wanted to 'amuse the fleet with a signal'. He planned to signal, *'England confides* [is confident] *that every man will do his duty'*, but Pasco suggested he use the word 'expects' instead. This made the signal quicker because 'expects' was a word in the official signal code and could be hoisted in just three flags rather than spelt out letter by letter.

THE ADMIRAL'S QUARTERS

Victory was usually in service as a 'flagship' meaning that she was the home of an Admiral in command of the whole fleet as well as of her Captain, who commanded the ship. Although life at sea could never be truly comfortable, with the constant damp and movement of the ship and the threat of sea sickness (from which even Nelson suffered), the Admiral at least had a light and spacious living space. Generally known as the Great Cabin, it occupies one quarter of the Upper Gun Deck and is actually in four separate parts.

The Day Cabin was the Admiral's office, where he planned battle strategy, commanded the fleet and wrote his dispatches.

It was at the breakfast table here that Nelson wrote his famous prayer before the Battle of Trafalgar. However, all is not as it seems; concealed in the 'quarter galleries' on both sides are 'seats of easement' or private toilet facilities. There are also gun ports, carefully hidden by bulkheads or seats, ready to be used when the ship was cleared for action so that even the Cabin became part of the fighting machine.

The elegant Dining Room was used by the Admiral to entertain senior officers in style. Outside is an ante-room, known as the Steerage (ships' tillers were once steered from this position), where the Admiral's valets and clerks gathered.

Left: The Admiral's Day Cabin.

Above: The Admiral's Dining Cabin.

Unlike Captain Hardy, who slept in a cot, Vice-Admiral Nelson chose to sleep in a campaign bed. This versatile piece of furniture was used as a chair during the day, folded out to form a small four-poster bed at night, and could be folded down to form a small table as required. Nearby is a reproduction of his dressing cabinet, made from the timbers of the *Foudroyant*, Nelson's flagship in the Mediterranean in 1799.

In February 1797, on the eve of the Battle of Cape St Vincent, Nelson (then a Commodore) dined in this cabin as a guest of Admiral Sir John Jervis, Commander-in-Chief of the Mediterranean Fleet. It was Nelson's decisive manoeuvre in HMS *Captain* that prevented the escape of the Spanish flagship during the battle and helped win the day. Nelson was knighted and promoted to Rear-Admiral soon afterwards.

Left: Steerage. The administrative burden on Nelson was immense; for example, on 29 September 1805, his 47th birthday, he spent seven hours writing orders and instructions.

THE UPPER GUN DECK

The Admiral's Quarters occupy just the stern of the Upper Gun Deck, often called the 'Main Deck'. The rest of this deck was a busy working area, the centre part of which was open to the elements, for the ship's craftsmen: the Carpenter's crew, Cooper, Ropemaker and Sailmakers. It also included a formidable battery of 30 long 12-pounder guns.

Further forward under the Foc'sle on the starboard side is the Sick Berth, where sailors were segregated from the rest of the crew to prevent the spread of disease. The sick men lay in hanging cots furnished with linen sheets, close to a dispensary and separate toilet facilities. When the *Victory* was in action the Sick Berth would be dismantled and moved to the Orlop Deck below the waterline.

Above: *Victory* carried six boats, four of which were stowed on skid beams in the ship's Waist. Working boats were painted in relatively dull colours of yellow, black and white, whereas the Admiral's Barge was more elaborately decorated in green and gold.

Above: The dispensary in *Victory*'s Sick Berth. Many medicines used at the time, such as antimony, are now regarded as dangerous poisons.

Guns took their individual names from the size of iron shot they used: a 12-pounder would fire a single iron ball weighing 12lb. However, other types of shot were used depending on the circumstances. Grapeshot, which was used against boats, was a bundle of small iron balls packed tightly together in a canvas bag. When fired the bag would be shredded and the balls separate to cause severe injuries. Bar shot (two balls joined by an iron bar) and chain shot (two balls linked with a chain) were designed to cut the rigging and spars at close quarters, though both could also slice a man's head clean from his body.

Above: The Sick Berth was located underneath the Forecastle, in a relatively bright and airy part of the ship. In battle it was dismantled, and casualties were treated below on the Orlop Deck.

THE MIDDLE GUN DECK

Towards the bow and at the heart of the Middle Gun Deck is the massive iron Brodie stove standing on thick tiles. This is the Galley area, the pantry for food preparation being screened off by wooden panels. More than 800 men were fed daily from here, with food cooked in ovens that could bake 80lb of bread and copper pans that would hold 250 gallons of stew at one time. The stove is named after Alexander Brodie, a Scottish master blacksmith who specialised in supplying stoves to the Navy.

The ship's normal daily routine was divided into seven 'watches' which were effectively a rota detailing which part of the crew was at work ('on watch') on deck. Afternoon Watch was from noon until 1600, followed by First Dog Watch, Last Dog Watch, First Watch, Middle Watch, Morning Watch and Forenoon Watch. Each period lasted four hours, apart from the two dog watches which were two hours each and enabled seamen to vary the rota.

Above: The starboard Entry Port.

The two large round wooden 'drumheads' on this deck are the upper parts of *Victory*'s two capstans, which were essential to raise and lower the ship's anchors, boats and guns. The main capstan, used for the anchors, is at the stern while the 'jeer' capstan (from the word 'gear') in the middle was used for all heavy stores and guns coming onboard, as well as for raising masts.

The hammocks slung between the guns on this deck belonged to the 142 Royal Marines, privates and non-commissioned officers, all of whom had volunteered. The other Marine officers lived and dined in the Wardroom at the stern. This provided the living quarters for most of the ship's officers, cabins leading off a central room with a shared dining table.

Right: The Galley Pantry. Food for *Victory*'s crew was prepared at the mess tables and brought to the Brodie stove to be cooked.

Above: The head of the jeer capstan.

It was considered unlucky to whistle on board ship – unless you were a cook. It was reassuring to hear cooks whistle because they could not whistle and spit in the food (or indeed eat it) at the same time!

THE LOWER GUN DECK

On the Lower Gun Deck the claustrophobia and discomfort of life on board a wooden battleship is most obvious. Here, amongst *Victory*'s heaviest guns (30 massive 32-pounders), 460 men slept and almost 600 took their meals.

At sea, with the gun ports lashed shut, the only natural light filtered dimly through gratings, and the men lived by candle and lantern light. They slept cheek-by-jowl in hammocks slung from the beams between the guns and arranged side by side, with each man allowed just 15 inches of space. They ate in messes of four or eight at tables either hung down from the deck head or unfolded across the deck.

At the stern, separated from the rest of the deck by a canvas screen, was the Gunroom. Here the Gunner, Chaplain and Midshipmen slept and ate in four canvas-walled cabins which were taken down when the deck was cleared for action. The youngest boys on the ship also lived here under the care of the Gunner.

Around the main mast which rises through this deck are four chain pumps which removed any water that had seeped into the Hold.

Each man on board *Victory* was issued with a hammock, two blankets and a mattress stuffed with wool. During the day the hammocks were rolled up and stowed in nets on the upper decks. Although the sleeping space was cramped, the watch system meant that at any one time half the crew might be working while the others slept.

Above: A typical mess table for eight seamen.

Above: The chain pumps, used for pumping water from the bilges.

The wooden manger at the bow end of the Lower Gun Deck was probably not used to house animals (although cattle, pigs, goats and chickens were all taken on board at times to provide fresh meat and eggs). Its purpose was to prevent water running along the deck as it came in through the 'hawse holes', the round holes through which the anchor cables entered the ship.

Left: Hammock cranes, where hammocks were stored on deck when not in use. Here they provided a defence against splinters in battle, and served as life preservers should a member of the crew fall overboard.

15

THE ORLOP DECK

The Orlop is the ship's lowest deck and gets its name because it literally 'overlaps' the Hold. The Orlop was below the waterline and therefore had no guns; there was even less height to stand up and the light was dimmer than on other decks.

The Orlop housed some of the specialists who were essential for keeping the *Victory* at sea. It was where the Surgeon carried out his grisly work in time of battle, and where 'standing officers' like the Carpenter and Boatswain lived in cramped and airless cabins.

Below: The Boatswain's Store. Ships like *Victory* were expected to be at sea for significant periods of time and carried extensive stores of rope, canvas and blocks with which to make running repairs.

It was the base for the Purser (in Nelson's time one William Burke) whose job was to provision the ship with food, drink, bedding, tobacco and some clothing. His Steward, whose responsibility was to measure out the daily rations to the 'mess cooks', was in charge of the 'rundles' or barrels of peas, oatmeal and bags of ship's biscuit. Cheeses on racks and flour for making bread were also stored here.

Right: *Victory's* After Cockpit provided an area where battle casualties might be operated upon.

Stores assistants in today's Royal Navy are still nicknamed 'Jack Dusty', a legacy of the days when the flour-covered Purser's Steward would be called 'Jack o'the Dust'.

Below: The Gunner's Store, where cutlasses, muskets and pikes were stored, along with spares for the ship's cannons and their carriages.

Right: The Cable Tier. Here *Victory's* seven anchor cables were stored.

THE HOLD

The Main and After Holds comprise a huge open space below the waterline. They were used to store the great quantities of provisions which were needed to keep *Victory* at sea for six months. Most things were kept in casks, with 'leaguers', the great water barrels holding 150 gallons, arranged as the bottom tier. On top of these were stacked casks which held up to 11,000 gallons of beer, 50 tons of salt beef and the same quantity of pork, and 15 tons of dried peas and two tons of butter. As casks were emptied they might be 'shaken down' and stored as separate wooden staves and iron hoops, or they might be refilled with water to help balance the ship.

The Hold also carried the ballast needed to counteract the great weight of guns and masts on *Victory*. This consisted of 257 tons of iron ingots covered with 200 tons of shingle pebbles. Under the direction of the ship's Master the crew could move the shingle in baskets in order to 'trim' the ship and improve her sailing qualities. The shingle also tended to smell as it soaked up sea water and leaks from the food casks so it had to be washed, fumigated or even replaced. Additional weight came from more than 100 tons of iron shot stored in special lockers in the Hold.

Left: The Main Hold. *Victory* carried provisions to support her crew of 820 for several months.

Above: The Grand Magazine Pallating Flat. Here 784 barrels, each containing 100lb of gunpowder, were stored.

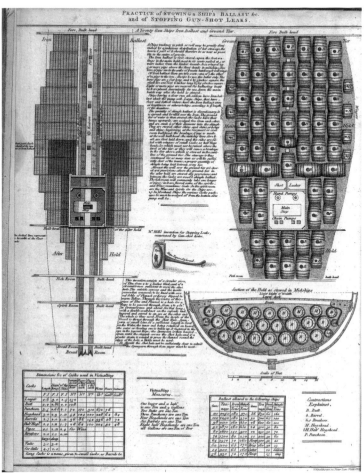

Above: Loading ballast and stores into a ship was a complicated exercise. The scale of the task is shown here in a contemporary set of instructions.

Left: The Grand Magazine Filling Room. Here gunpowder was bagged in order to create charges for the ship's cannon. Barrels of gunpowder were emptied into the trough, and the powder scooped into bags.

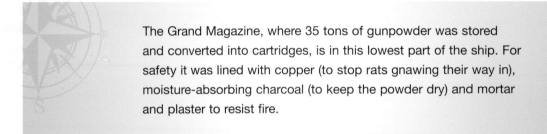

The Grand Magazine, where 35 tons of gunpowder was stored and converted into cartridges, is in this lowest part of the ship. For safety it was lined with copper (to stop rats gnawing their way in), moisture-absorbing charcoal (to keep the powder dry) and mortar and plaster to resist fire.

THE CREW

At the time of Trafalgar, *Victory* had a crew of 820 men. It would have been possible to sail and manoeuvre the ship with far fewer, but large numbers were needed to man her guns and fight in battle. From the Admiral like Nelson, down to the 31 boys on board, each person had a distinct role to play.

The ship's Captain and nine commissioned officers were in overall charge of the ship and the crew, whilst warrant officers like the Boatswain, Carpenter, Gunner, Surgeon and Purser were specialists responsible for a single aspect. The Master, for example, looked after navigation and the ship's log. The Royal Marines provided the ship's fighting force and numbered 11 officers and 135 privates.

The great majority of the crew – over 500 – were the seamen who sailed or fought on the ship. These men were rated (and paid) according to their skill and experience: from the 70 skilled 'petty officers', through the 212 experienced 'able seamen' and the 193 useful 'ordinary seamen', right down to the 87 landsmen – who were without previous experience of the sea.

Above: A typical seaman of the Georgian Royal Navy standing on the Fore Channel of a ship. The seaman is holding a lead line, which was used in shallow or unknown waters to ascertain the depth of water under a ship's keel, and ensure it did not run aground.

PRIZE MONEY.

ALL Shares not paid by the Agents, within four Months after the first Distribution, are transmitted to Greenwich Hospital; and all Persons entitled thereto, may receive the same by personal Application or by Letter, addressed to the Clerk of the Check, Royal Hospital, Greenwich, **without the Assistance of any Agent, and without Risk or Expense;** The Certificates of Service must be produced, or transmitted, at the time of Application.

By the Commissioners for Executing the Office of Lord High Admiral of Great Britain and Ireland, &c. and of all His Majesty's Plantations, &c.

IN Pursuance of His Majesty's Order in Council, dated the 14th Day of December, 1796, We do hereby Impower and Direct you to Impress, or cause to be Impressed, so many Seamen, Seafaring Men, and Persons whose Occupations and Callings are to work in Vessels and Boats upon Rivers, as shall be necessary either to man His Majesty's Ship under your Command, or any other of His Majesty's Ships, giving unto each Man so Impressed One Shilling for Prest Money. And, in the Execution hereof, you are to take Care, that neither yourself, nor any Officer authorized by you, do demand or receive any Money, Gratuity, Reward, or other Consideration whatsoever, for the Sparing, Exchanging or Discharging, any Person or Persons Impressed or to be Impressed, as you will answer it at your Peril.—You are not to intrust any Person with the Execution of this Warrant but a Commission Officer, and to insert his Name and Office in the Deputation on the other Side hereof, and set your Hand and Seal thereto.—This Warrant to continue in Force till the Thirty-first Day of December, 1797. And, in the due Execution thereof, all Mayors, Sheriffs, Justices of the Peace, Bailiffs, Constables, Headboroughs, and all other His Majesty's Officers and Subjects whom it may concern, are hereby required to be aiding and assisting unto you, and those employed by you, as they tender His Majesty's Service, and will answer the contrary at their Perils. Given under our Hands, and the Seal of the Office of Admiralty, the 1st Day of May 1797.

To
Captain John Tho' Duckworth
Commander of His Majesty's Ship
the Leviathan —

By Command of their Lordships,

For these men, living and working at sea was dangerous: it is estimated that 90 per cent of the 92,000 British fatalities during the wars with France were caused by disease, accident and shipwreck. However, many of the aspects of life at sea which appear harsh to us, such as child labour and corporal punishment, were also part of life ashore. Navy service was attractive in many ways. Although basic pay was relatively low (23s. 6d. a month for an ordinary seaman in 1805) compared to that of merchant seamen, the crew were guaranteed regular food and drink and had the chance of prize money. Experienced sailors would have been aware that, with many more men aboard, their duties were actually lighter than on merchant ships. The old belief that *Victory*'s sailors were forced to serve by the Press Gang, or were convicted criminals who chose to serve in the Navy rather than sit in gaol, is too simplistic. Among the crew at Trafalgar were 289 volunteers, as against 217 who had been pressed into service, and no one at all who was recruited from prison.

Seamen learned their trade early and *Victory*'s crew was overwhelmingly young. Approximately 40 per cent were under 24 and the youngest boy onboard was 12 (though for good measure the Purser, who was the oldest crew member, was 67). This was also a multi-national crew of seafarers, with one in ten coming from outside the British Isles (from places like the United States, Canada, mainland Europe and even India).

EATING AND DRINKING

It was important that *Victory*'s provisions remained edible through the many months at sea. Therefore the crew's diet was limited and repetitive, made up of staples which had proved to last well, such as salted beef and pork, dried biscuit, peas and oatmeal, butter and cheese. These were stored in casks or bread bags in the Hold, but inevitably some went bad as barrels leaked, were infested by weevils or eaten by rats.

In harbour the diet was better and more varied, with soft bread and fresh meat. By the time of Trafalgar the disease of scurvy – which we now know was caused by lack of vitamin C in the diet – had largely been overcome by efforts to provide regular fresh vegetables and add lemon juice to the rum ration. Overall the diet was generous and high in calories, vital to sustain the crew in their hard, physical work.

The men's daily ration included eight pints of beer, though if they were serving away from home waters this might be replaced by two pints of wine, or a half-pint of rum. This was a practical solution to the problem of thirst since stored water was very bulky and rapidly became unfit for drinking.

Men ate as part of a 'mess' which they chose themselves. This usually contained eight men, one of whom was appointed 'mess cook' for a week and took on the work of receiving, preparing and collecting their provisions. There was usually only one hot meal a day so breakfast might be a dish like 'burgoo', an oatmeal porridge sweetened with molasses. Any actual cooking was done under the supervision of the ship's cook on *Victory*'s single iron stove, which included coppers for boiling, roasting spits and a bread oven.

Left: Ship's cooks were usually older men who had perhaps lost a limb, rendering them unfit for the more physical aspects of a life at sea.

Above: Leave was rarely given to the men of the Lower Deck due to the risk of desertion and so when in harbour women, usually described as 'wives', became a common sight on board ship.

Right: The amount of food allowed to each man was clearly set down in the Navy's regulations.

(61)

Of the Provisions.

Article I.

THERE shall be allowed to every Man serving in His Majesty's Ships, a daily Proportion of Provisions, according as is expressed in the following Table, *viz.* *Allowance of Provisions.*

	Bifcuit Pounds Averdupoiz.	Beer Gallons Wine Meafure.	Beef Pounds Averdupoiz.	Pork Pounds Averdupoiz.	Peafe Pint Winchefter Meafure.	Oatmeal Pint Winchefter Meafure.	Butter Ounces.	Cheefe Ounces.
Sunday -	1	1			1 half.			
Monday --	1	1				1	2	4
Tuefday --	1	1	2					
Wednefday -	1	1			1 half.	1	2	4
Thurfday --	1	1		1	1 half.			
Friday ---	1	1			1 half.	1	2	4
Saturday --	1	1	2					

II.

It is left to the Difcretion of the Commanders of Squadrons to fhorten the aforefaid Allowance of Provifions, according to the Exigence of the Service, taking Care that the Men be punctually paid for the fame. The like Power is given to Captains of fingle Ships, in Cafes of abfolute Neceffity; but the Purfer is ftrictly charged not to fupply any Officer at whole Allowance, whilft the reft of the Company are at fhort; but all are to be equal in Point of Victualling. *May be fhortned, when the Service require it.*

III. In

DISCIPLINE AND PUNISHMENT

The constant 'discipline' required to organise the crew on a ship as complex as *Victory* and run her in a safe, efficient way should not be confused with the occasional 'punishment' meted out to the few.

The crew were disciplined and organised in a number of ways. They were placed in one of two (or occasionally three) watches and this determined when they had to work and literally be 'on watch'. For the more complex activities onboard, such as mooring, raising the anchor or tacking the ship, each man was given a 'station' or a specific place to work. He was also allocated a 'quarter' for fighting on the ship, which might be in a gun crew or one of the magazines

Left: The cat o'nine tails was a common form of punishment in the sailing navy. Often left to the discretion of the Captain, the number of lashes could vary from 12 to 36.

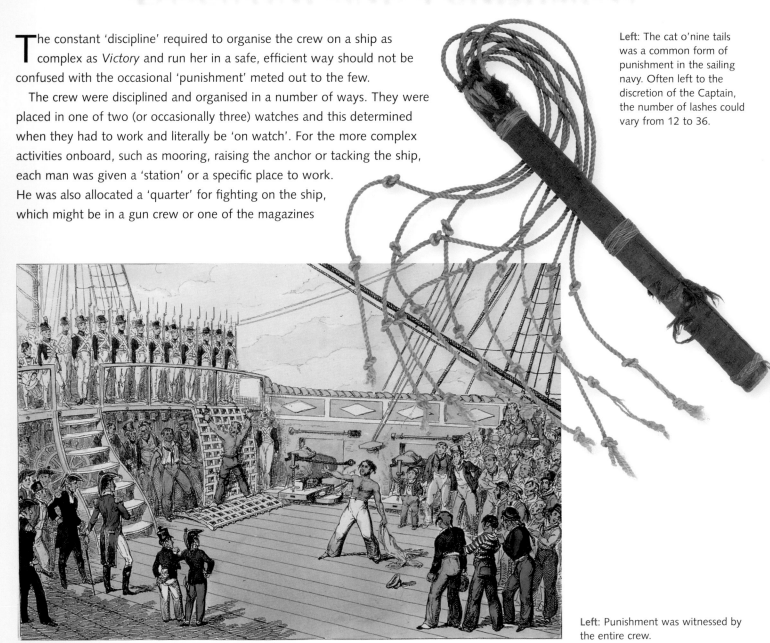

Left: Punishment was witnessed by the entire crew.

or involve working aloft. The ship's 10 commissioned officers and 21 Midshipmen were responsible for a small 'division' of men and supervised their health and welfare.

Overall the crew were relatively lightly disciplined in military terms. Although they dressed in standard loose trousers and short blue jackets they did not have an official uniform. With so few commissioned officers on board their life on the Mess Deck was lightly policed.

When things went wrong the Captain had a range of punishments at his disposal. Most commonly he awarded anything from 12 to 36 lashes for offences like drunkenness, insolence or neglect of duty. This excruciatingly painful punishment was carried out by the Boatswain's Mates, offenders being brought to the Quarter Deck in front of the ship's company, stripped to the waist and tied to an upturned wooden grating. A seaman caught thieving was made to 'run the gauntlet' past fellow crewmen who beat him with knotted rope ends. Others would be locked into leg irons (or 'bilboes') on the Main Gun Deck, eating only bread and water. Midshipmen, the Navy's young trainee officers, were caned rather than flogged if punished, or could be 'mast-headed' – sent aloft to sit at the head of the mast in the wind and cold.

The most severe punishments for offences like mutiny or desertion were awarded by courts martial. Men 'flogged round the fleet' could receive up to 300 lashes, which were often fatal; others were hung from the yard.

THE SHIP'S SPECIALISTS

The Gunner, Carpenter and Boatswain were *Victory*'s specialists and knew the ship inside out. They were known as 'standing officers' because they stayed with a ship whether it was in active service or laid up in the harbour 'in ordinary'. This meant that they often had a very long service on the ship. William Rivers, for example, was *Victory*'s Gunner for 20 years from 1793 to 1812.

Each had responsibility for valuable stores and tools and directed a crew of artisans equipped with the skills essential to keeping the ship at sea and in fighting condition. The Carpenter made repairs to the hull, fittings and equipment, including the masts and spars. The Caulker worked for him, using oakum to keep the decks watertight, as did the Cooper, who constantly remade and repaired the casks which stored food and water.

The Gunner had the largest crew and, perhaps, the greatest responsibility because the risk of devastating explosion from the ship's magazines was always there. Assisted by Gunner's Mates, Quarter Gunners and the Yeoman of the Powder Room, he looked after the great guns and their fittings, as well as the different types of shot and powder. He also directed the Armourer and the Gunsmith, who maintained muskets, bayonets, pistols, cutlasses, pikes and boarding axes.

The Boatswain's duty was to care for the standing and running rigging, blocks, sails, cables and anchors. He had a specialist Sailmaker and Ropemaker to assist with repairs as well as Boatswain's Mates who would supervise the seamen.

Above: The Armourer's tools and anvil allowed repairs to be made to most metal fittings on board the ship.

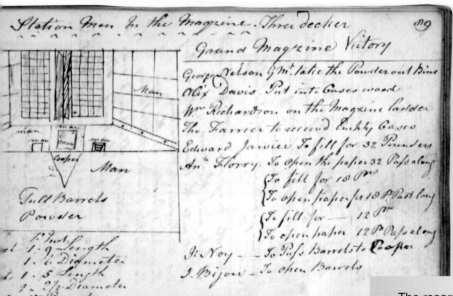

Left: The Carpenter's Store Room also doubled as a workshop space.

The records kept by Gunner Rivers show that during the Battle of Trafalgar HMS *Victory* fired 3,041 shot and expended 7.5 tons of gunpowder, 3 tons of junk wads, 3,000 musket balls and 1,000 pistol shot.

THE ROYAL MARINES

The Marines on board *Victory* ('Royal Marines' from 1802) were a separate force from the main crew. They looked different in their distinctive red and white uniforms, and ate and slept separately on the Middle Gun Deck, keeping themselves apart from the seaman.

They were a professional military unit of sea-based soldiers, more like the Army than the Navy in many ways. Men volunteered to join the Marines; they were never press-ganged and were commanded by their own officers. On the *Victory* a Captain of Marines shared the Wardroom with the naval officers.

At sea they would join the seamen in hauling ropes and turning the capstan, but regulations ordered that they were 'not obliged to go aloft, or to be beat or punished for not showing an inclination to do so'. The Marines were at the sharp end of any fighting with other ships, whether as part of a gun crew, firing muskets or in boarding parties. Increasingly they also took part in amphibious actions, using the ship's boats to go ashore and to 'cut out' enemy vessels in raids.

The Marines also had a key role in policing the ship. They guarded sensitive areas, like the Spirit Room which stored alcohol, and stood sentinel outside the officers' quarters. After the great mutinies at Spithead (off Portsmouth) and the Nore (off the Thames) in 1797 they were given a greater role in maintaining discipline and preventing dissent amongst the seamen.

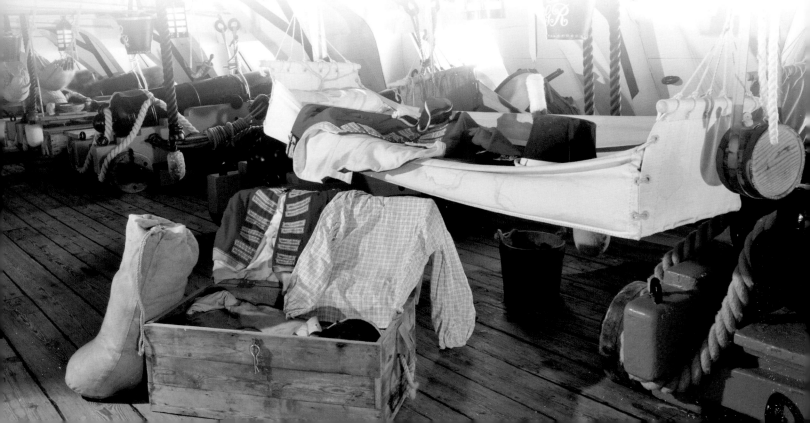

Above: Royal Marine drummers were responsible for beating *Victory*'s crew to their quarters in preparation for battle.

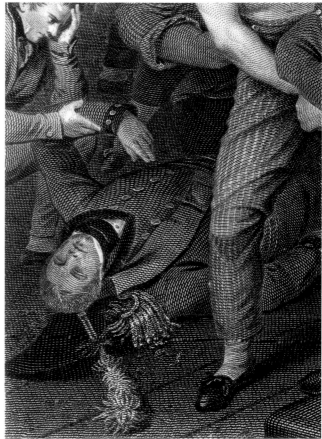

Above: Captain of Marines Charles Adair was shot and killed during the Battle of Trafalgar, sharing Nelson's fate.

Captain of Marines Charles Adair showed great bravery at Trafalgar. As the French warship *Redoubtable* came close alongside, he stood on *Victory*'s gangway, encouraging his fighting men to repel the French boarders. He shared the same fate as Nelson and was killed by a musket ball fired from the *Redoubtable*.

HORATIO NELSON

The achievements of Nelson's long naval career are sometimes obscured by his dazzling victory and poignant death at Trafalgar. Yet by 1805 he had already served in the Navy for 34 years, been wounded many times and fought in three major fleet actions.

Horatio Nelson was born in 1758, the son of a country clergyman from Norfolk. The family were not wealthy, but were well connected and his uncle Captain Maurice Suckling was able to take him on his ship the *Raisonnable* as a Midshipman when he was just 12 years old. This early experience at sea was vital and enabled Nelson to pass his examination for Lieutenant six years later and be made 'Post Captain' at just 20. From the age of 21 he spent almost eight continuous years in independent command of frigates, fighting ships that were much smaller than *Victory*.

He first came to public notice with his daring boarding and capture of two Spanish ships at the Battle of Cape St Vincent in 1797. The whole of Europe learned his name the following year

Above: Nelson receiving the surrendered sword of a Spanish captain following the Battle of Cape St Vincent (14 February 1797).

Nelson met the young widow Francis Nesbit when he was commanding HMS *Boreas* in the West Indies. They married in 1787 and made their home in his native Norfolk. After he went to sea again in 1793 they did not meet for another four years, and a year later in Naples he became close to Emma Hamilton, wife of William Hamilton, the British Envoy. A love affair started that lasted the rest of his life, resulting eventually in separation from his wife and the birth of a daughter Horatia in 1801.

Above: A contemporary caricature produced following the Battle of the Nile. Nelson is shown destroying French Revolutionary crocodiles with a club of 'British Oak'.

when he commanded the fleet which won a devastating victory over the French at the Battle of the Nile and turned the tide against Napoleon's military success.

This all came at a heavy personal cost. Nelson suffered a number of wounds in battle, the most severe being the loss of sight in one eye at Calvi in Corsica, the loss of his right arm at Santa Cruz in Tenerife, and a head wound in Egypt. Conditions at sea also took their toll, and his steward on *Victory* wrote in 1805, 'That good man was upon deck, maimed as he is, sometime half naked under such heavy rains as are never seen in England, it is no wonder his Lordship is rather shook and I am afraid he will not mend here for half the time he is deprived of the common necessaries of life.'

Above and below: Nelson met Emma Hamilton whilst serving in the Mediterranean, and the two embarked upon a love affair that was to see the birth of a daughter and last until Nelson's death.

Following Trafalgar, Emma quickly fell into debt and moved to France to escape creditors. She died there in 1815.

Left: Whilst personally leading an amphibious attack on Tenerife, Nelson was wounded in the arm by a musket ball. He was rowed back to his ship where the Surgeon removed most of the right arm.

CAPTAIN THOMAS HARDY

When there was an Admiral on board the Captain of *Victory* was known as the 'Flag Captain'. He was responsible for the ship but was often relatively junior compared to other captains of ships of the line.

In 1805 Thomas Masterman Hardy was Flag Captain. He was 10 years younger than Nelson, temperamentally much calmer and physically much taller. It has been said that 'By nature he was calm, patient, slow and careful ... In figure he was broad and massive; his features, as he grew older, had the strength and bluntness of the old Romans; he had a chin like a battering ram ...'. The difference in their sizes is clearly shown by his cot; it hangs in the Captain's Cabin and dwarfs that of Nelson.

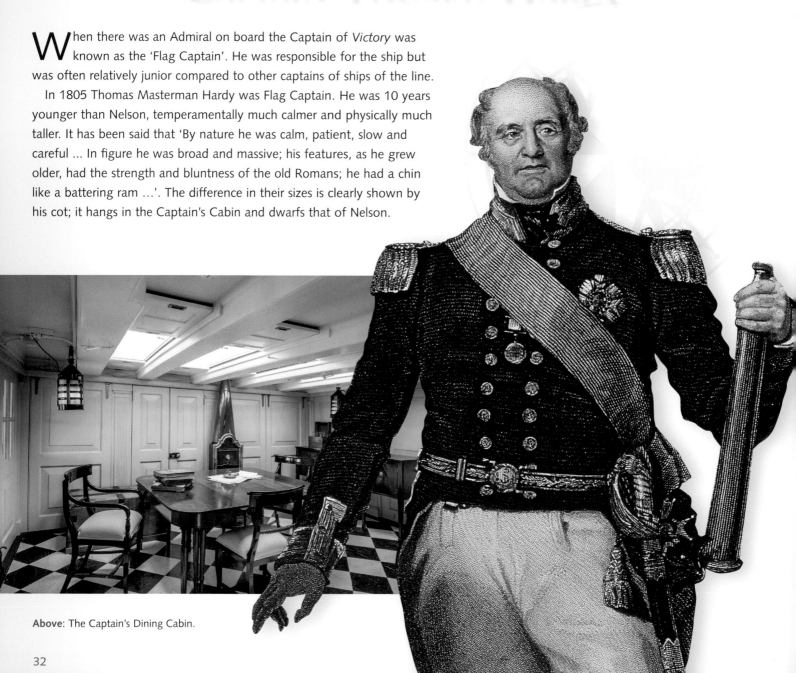

Above: The Captain's Dining Cabin.

By the time of Trafalgar they had known each other for 12 years, and for much of that time Hardy relied on Nelson to be the patron who advanced his career. He was a junior member of the captains who made up Nelson's celebrated 'Band of Brothers'. He was present at all Nelson's major fleet actions and had been chosen as his Flag Captain for the first time in 1798 following the Battle of the Nile.

Hardy continued to serve after the Battle of Trafalgar. As late as the 1820s he was Commander-in-Chief in South America, and then he became First Sea Lord and later Governor of Greenwich Hospital. He died in 1839.

Hardy said the two men worked so well together because whenever Nelson wished to be an Admiral Hardy would act as his Flag Captain, but if Nelson wanted to play the Captain Hardy was content to be his First Lieutenant.

Left: *Death of Nelson* by Arthur William Devis. Hardy is shown standing behind the group crouched around Nelson.

THE LONG CAMPAIGN

The Battle of Trafalgar was the culmination of a long and complex naval campaign.

In March 1805 a French fleet sailed out of Toulon, managing to elude Nelson's blockading ships. Commanded by Admiral Pierre de Villeneuve, the fleet gathered Spanish ships and sailed to the West Indies. The plan was to rendezvous with further French forces and create a fleet large enough to enter the English Channel and support Napoleon's 'Grand Armée', which was assembling to invade Britain.

After searching in the Mediterranean Nelson gave chase, and by early June he was in the Caribbean hot on Villeneuve's

Left: When Nelson explained his plan to the captains of the fleet, the impact was dramatic: 'some shed tears, all approved, as it was new, it was singular, it was simple'.

'Something must be left to chance; nothing is sure in a sea fight above all others. Shot will carry away the masts and yards of friends as well as foes ... Captains are to look to their particular Lines as their rallying point. But in case signals can neither be seen or perfectly understood, no Captain can do very wrong if he places his ship alongside that of an enemy.' (Nelson's Trafalgar Memorandum, written on 9 October 1805)

Above: The Admiralty Board Room in London, from where the Lord Commissioners of the Admiralty managed the Royal Navy.

Left: Britain's Prime Minister William Pitt seated opposite Emperor Napoleon. Between them they are carving up the world; Pitt taking the oceans and Napoleon Europe.

' ... you will duly appreciate the importance of this communication when I inform you that if you tell me the Enemy's fleet are not at Trinidada, that I shall stand immediately for Grenada and therefore that I must not unnecessarily be carried to Leeward.' (Letter sent by Nelson on 6 June during the search for the French Fleet)

trail. He was able to send intelligence back to the Admiralty so that after Villeneuve re-crossed the Atlantic he was met by a squadron of ships under Sir Robert Calder and forced to turn south and seek refuge in Spanish ports. This effectively frustrated Napoleon's plans for an invasion of Britain, so that when Nelson re-joined the fleet in September Villeneuve was already planning to sail into the Mediterranean.

With the Combined Fleet bottled up in Cadiz, Nelson brought his captains together and outlined his battle plan. This was to split his fleet into two columns and isolate the rear of the enemy's line, bringing on what he called 'a pell-mell battle'. Each commander knew his ship's place in the line and how to react.

Early in the morning of 21 October the enemy were finally sighted at sea; crews raced to clear for action and take their quarters.

CLEARING FOR ACTION, BEATING TO QUARTERS

On the call to 'Clear for Action' the crew started a well-drilled routine to remove anything which might get in the way or cause deadly splinters during battle. Wooden bulkheads or partitions within the ship were moved, and mess tables on the lower decks were cleared. The officers' furniture was wrapped and stowed in the Hold, the stern windows removed and the stern chaser guns put in position. The sails were secured and safety nets hung to catch anything that might fall on the men below. The ship's boats were lowered and towed astern. Sails, boom, boats and hammock rolls were doused with water to prevent their being set alight. Fire buckets were filled and hoses laid, while wet sand was sprinkled on deck to prevent men slipping.

Once in sight of the enemy the Royal Marine drummers 'Beat to Quarters' as a signal for the crew to take up their action stations. This might be anywhere from the fighting tops to the Orlop Deck, but the great majority were part of a gun crew.

Each 32-pounder gun usually had a seven man crew to load and fire it, plus a powder monkey who carried flannel bags of gunpowder. The speed of gun crews gave the British a real advantage in action, and a well-trained crew could load, aim and fire a gun in just 90 seconds. To load the gun

Above: Although the Admiral's Quarters are finely panelled, this material was removable to allow cannons to be mounted in the area during battle.

One of *Victory*'s crew, Able Seaman Benjamin Stevenson, wrote to his sister after the Battle of Trafalgar:

'Dear Sister we had a very hard engagement with them indeed it lasted 4 hours and a half constant fire but thank god we had the good fortune to gain the Victory…After the prisoners came on board they sayed that the Devil loaded the guns for it was impossible for man to load and fire so Quick as we did.'

a long corkscrew 'worm' was first used to clear debris from the muzzle and a wet sheepskin sponge then pushed in to make sure all embers were extinguished. Next a powder bag was rammed down the muzzle into the breech of the gun, followed by a wad of rope yarn, the all-important shot and another wad. The Gun Captain then pierced the gunpowder bag through the 'touch-hole', and the powder was ignited either by a lighted match or, increasingly, by gun-locks which were safer and faster to use.

On firing, the gun and its carriage, weighing many tons, recoiled viciously, restrained only by men holding breeching ropes. The noise was deafening and blinding smoke filled the gun decks.

Right: *Victory* carried 150 muskets.

Right: At Trafalgar *Victory*'s cannon were equipped with gun locks (right) that used a flint to generate a spark. In battle the flints would quickly become blunt and so a slow match held in a linstock (below right) was provided as a back up.

THE BATTLE

The day of 21 October was clear with light winds, which brought the two fleets together at a walking pace. The British fleet was split into two columns and sailing directly towards the French and Spanish ships, so it was the ships leading each line – HMS *Royal Sovereign* under the command of Admiral Collingwood and HMS *Victory* under Nelson – which faced the devastating force of their initial broadsides.

As Collingwood attacked the rear, Nelson smashed through the centre of the line. *Victory* delivered a knockout blow on Villeneuve's flagship, the *Bucentaur*, and was then locked in combat at point blank range with the *Redoubtable*. This created a gap, and the ships astern of *Victory* poured through to engage

Left: Nelson's plan called for the British fleet to be split into two columns, smashing through the enemy line and dividing it into three sections.

Right: Nelson succeeded in bringing on a 'pell mell battle' in which the better organisation and greater rate of fire of British ships overwhelmed the enemy fleet.

Left: Nelson supervised the British fleet from the Quarter Deck of HMS *Victory*. This was an exposed and dangerous position – Nelson's secretary John Scott and several Marines were killed before Nelson himself was shot.

A man's chances of survival depended largely upon where he was stationed in the ship. After the battle, *Victory*'s Chaplain Alexander Scott reported, 'On the Quarter Deck, Poop and Forecastle the slaughter was immense; on the other decks, comparatively nothing; on the lower deck only two wounded, and strange to tell, by musket balls.'

and overwhelm the French. The battle which began at midday was over by 4.30 that afternoon. The plan Nelson conceived in advance was an overwhelming success; his fleet of 27 ships defeated a French and Spanish force of 33, capturing 17 ships and setting one ablaze.

However, the victory came at great cost. Nelson himself was hit by a musket ball fired from the *Redoutable* when the action was at its height. The ball entered at his left shoulder and cut through a lung and a major artery before hitting his spine. He was carried to the Orlop Deck where he died three hours later after suffering great pain. Casualties were heavy: *Victory* lost 57 men and had 102 injured. Across the British fleet nearly 500 men died, whilst in the Combined Fleet more than 3,000 lost their lives.

THE AFTERMATH

Shortly after the battle a severe storm blew up. Exhausted crews that had suffered many casualties, and severe damage to ships, meant a tremendous effort was required to get the fleet safely to port. Conditions were so dangerous that many of the ships captured from the French and Spanish, which had been taken under tow, had to be cut adrift. These prizes, which were valuable not just to the Navy but to the men themselves, were lost.

Victory had been severely damaged in the battle. With her masts and rigging shot through she was taken under tow to Gibraltar by the frigate HMS *Euryalus*. In Gibraltar her wounded men were landed and taken to the naval hospital, whilst the ship underwent emergency repairs. *Victory* returned to Portsmouth in December 1805 carrying Nelson's body preserved in a cask of brandy.

Admiral Collingwood's despatch, with news of an overwhelming victory, was carried to Britain in the fast schooner

Below: During the battle HMS *Victory* was badly damaged, losing her mizzen mast. Along with the rest of the British fleet she sailed to Gibraltar in order to make temporary repairs before returning to England.

Below: HMS *Victory*, carrying Nelson's body, moored off the Isle of Wight in December 1805.

HMS *Pickle*. Public rejoicing was tempered by mourning for Nelson's death and a great state funeral was planned. In January 1806 Nelson's body was carried up the Thames from Greenwich Naval Hospital to Whitehall, then a great procession which included sailors from the *Victory* took it to a burial service at St Paul's Cathedral.

Right: On HMS *Victory*'s return to England, many artists rushed to make sketches of the ship in order to ensure their paintings were as accurate as possible.

Below: Nelson's funeral in St Paul's Cathedral. Several thousand people were in attendance.

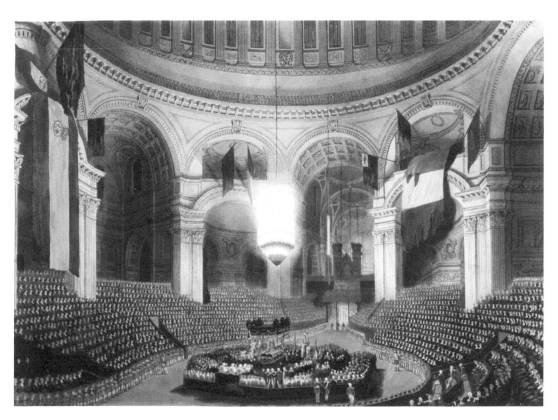

'The hull is much damaged by shot in a number of different places ... Several beams, knees and riders shot through and broke ... The mizzen mast shot away about nine feet above the deck; the mainmast shot through and sprung; the main yard gone ... the ship makes in bad weather 12 inches an hour.' (Just part of the damage to *Victory* described in the remark book of Midshipman Roberts, 1805)

VICTORY AFTER TRAFALGAR

Following Trafalgar, *Victory*, now tattered and battered, was put into reserve at Chatham and classed as a second-rate ship. This was not quite the end of her active service, however, and in 1808 she was re-commissioned to lead a fleet to the Baltic. An alliance between the French and Russians was excluding British ships from vital sources of hemp, flax and pine, all essential supplies for shipping. Sweden, which opposed this new alliance, needed British support, so a revitalised *Victory*, carrying the flag of Admiral Sir James Saumarez, kept the northern waters open to trade.

By 1812 she was no longer needed in this role, and her active career ended on 7 November when she was moored in Portsmouth Harbour. In 1814 she was brought into dry dock for a moderate repair, which soon became a significant refit, and much of the ship as she is seen today dates from this period. The refit included the replacement of many of the decks and the introduction of iron brackets to add strength to the ship's structure, along with substantial changes to the exterior, including alterations to the masts. The ship's

Below: *Victory* was rammed by HMS *Neptune* on 23 October 1903.

Right: Admiral Sir James Saumarez, who used *Victory* as his flagship in the Baltic.

Above: *Victory* c.1860. In the background can be seen HMS *Duke of Wellington*, which replaced *Victory* as flagship of the Port Admiral of Portsmouth between 1869 and 1891.

Above right: *Victory* on moorings at Gosport in the late 19th century.

Right: *Victory* in dry dock in 1905.

bow was rebuilt, reflecting changed ideas about strength and fighting ability following the experiences of 20 years of war.

From 1823–24 *Victory* was refitted as a 21-gun Guard ship and stationed in Portsmouth Harbour, where she continued to carry out useful functions – as a residence, a flagship and a tender providing accommodation. She did this for the next 80 years, as the Navy around her changed from timber sailing ships to steel-hulled, steam-powered dreadnoughts.

In 1903 HMS *Neptune*, a 9,000-ton steel battleship, broke loose while being towed from Portsmouth Harbour and rammed into the side of *Victory*. The damage and subsequent repair occurred just before the centenary of Trafalgar and drew attention to the poor condition of the ship, a condition that deteriorated during the First World War as money was concentrated on the Royal Navy's modern fighting ships. By 1921 it was feared that *Victory* would sink at her moorings in Portsmouth Harbour, and the decision was made to place her permanently in dry dock, where she remains today.

RESTORATION AND PRESERVATION

Throughout her active service *Victory* was regularly modified and repaired, her timbers and fittings often replaced. Changes were made to her hull, her armament and her decoration on many occasions. This process of change and renewal continued after she was moored in the Harbour and after her placement in dry dock in 1922.

Early approaches to the preservation of *Victory* in dry dock focused on restoring the ship to her Trafalgar appearance. This often involved the removal of parts dating to the Victorian period, which means we know relatively little about the ship's internal layout and appearance during most of the 19th century. Today the focus is on the conservation of the ship's historic material, rather than its replacement or removal, so we can better understand the full history of *Victory*, as well as the role she played at Trafalgar.

Above: HMS *Victory* undergoing restoration in the 1920s.

Right: A magnified cross-section of a paint sample from *Victory*, used to establish how the ship was painted at the time of the Battle of Trafalgar.

Above: A carpenter's race knife mark dating to 1815 on the underside of an Orlop Deck beam.

Left: A detailed 3D model of *Victory* constructed from a laser scan survey of the ship.

The increased focus on the conservation of the ship has involved the use of archaeological techniques such as tree-ring dating and a detailed study of the ship's timbers to help identify and understand important features within her structure. Microscopic analysis of *Victory*'s paint layers has helped to establish her true colours at Trafalgar, leading to her striking new appearance. These techniques help to protect and preserve the most significant aspects of the ship.

The repair and maintenance of *Victory* is a continual process, with the ship's timbers at risk of damage from the weather, rot, death watch beetle, and wear and tear from the hundreds of thousands of visitors that pass through her each year. Caring for *Victory* involves both traditional shipwrights' approaches to maintain her and keep her watertight, as well as the application of new techniques, such as a detailed 3D laser scanning of the ship to provide an understanding of her structure and to help develop new methods for supporting her in the future. This consideration of new materials and techniques will ensure that *Victory* is preserved for generations to come.

Victory's History, 1811–Present

1811	transports troops to Portugal
1812	end of active service – *Victory* is moored in Portsmouth Harbour
1824–30	used as flagship of the Port Admiral for the first time
1869–91	used as a tender to HMS *Duke of Wellington*
1893	fitted with iron masts taken from HMS *Shah*
1903	rammed and severely damaged by HMS *Neptune*
1922	enters dock – restoration guided by the Society for Nautical Research (SNR)
1928	repairs complete, the ship is opened to the public
1939	closed to the public
1941	bomb damaged
1955	start of another 'Great Repair'
1980	completion of her stern decoration
2009	celebrates 250th anniversary of laying of her keel
2012	custodianship of the ship transferred to the National Museum of the Royal Navy.

In 1941 *Victory* was damaged by an act of war once more. A German bomb smashed into the dock damaging her keel. The Germans claimed they had destroyed *Victory*, a renowned symbol of British might, but the Admiralty was quickly able to prove that they were stretching the truth.

FUTURE CONSERVATION

A wooden ship is designed to float. *Victory*, however, has been in dry dock for almost a century. This has caused the ship's hull to sag between the supporting cradles. Over the next few years the National Museum of the Royal Navy will be introducing a new support designed to prevent further deterioration of the ship's structure. The large cradles on which the ship sits will be replaced by 134 individual props positioned to support the ship's frames, allowing a clearer view of the ship below the waterline. This new support system will reduce the stresses in *Victory*'s hull and replicate the support offered by water when the ship was afloat.

Once the new support system is installed, a major conservation project will begin to ensure *Victory*'s survival for future generations. These are the first steps in an ongoing programme of conservation and preservation of the ship that will last for 15 years.

Above: The steel cradles that help to support *Victory* were installed in 1922 and were heavily modified throughout the 20th century.

Above: An artist's impression of the proposed new support system for *Victory*, consisting of 134 individual steel props.